BAKING FOR YOUR DOG

TASTY TREATS FOR YOUR FOUR-LEGGED FRIEND

Ingeborg Pils

Bath · New York · Singapore · Hong Kong · Cologne · Delhi · Melbourne

All recipes in this book have been carefully put together with advice from veterinary surgeons and tried out on different dogs. However, it is not impossible that in individual cases some meals may have negative consequences.
The publishers and the author can accept no liability for such consequences.

Not everything that human beings like to consume is good for dogs. Indisputably harmful are alcohol, cocoa, garlic, raisins, the onion family, chocolate with a high proportion of cocoa butter, raw pork, and hot spicy dishes. A few studies and Internet pages now classify further foodstuffs as poorly tolerated by dogs.

Other sources—the veterinary surgeons we consulted among them—disagree with these opinions.
If you are in any way uncertain how well your dog will tolerate any of the ingredients, please consult your veterinary surgeon.

This is a Parragon Publishing Book

This edition published in 2009

Parragon Publishing, Queen Street House, 4 Queen Street, Bath BA1 1HE, UK

Production: ditter.projektagentur GmbH; **Project coordination:** Michael Ditter; **Food photography:** Jo Kirchherr; **Food styling:** Rafael Pranschke; **Illustrations:** Kyra Stempell; **Design:** Sabine Vonderstein; **Lithography:** Klausner Medien Service GmbH

US edition produced by Cambridge Publishing Management Ltd
Project editor: Diane Teillol; **Translator:** Sue James; **Copy editor:** Sandra Stafford; **Typesetter:** Donna Pedley; **Proofreader:** Ian Faulkner

This book uses both imperial and metric measurements. Follow the same units of measurement throughout; do not mix imperial and metric. All spoon measurements are level: teaspoons are assumed to be 5 ml, and tablespoons are assumed to be 15 ml. Unless otherwise stated, milk is assumed to be whole, eggs and individual vegetables such as potatoes are medium, and pepper is freshly ground black pepper.

The times given are an approximate guide only. Preparation times differ according to the techniques used by different people and the cooking times may also vary from those given as a result of the type of oven used. Optional ingredients, variations, or serving suggestions have not been included in the calculations.

ISBN: 978-1-4075-4812-8

Printed in China

Contents

Introduction

Baking is love—these words, from an advertising slogan of the last century, may seem a bit exaggerated to many readers when applied to the well-being of our four-legged friends. However, baking always has something to do with warmth, closeness, and affection.

When the scent of Pauline's cheese dreams or Linda's liver sausage cookies emanates from my kitchen and fills the house, my four-legged housemate Dexter becomes very lively and will not leave his observation post just outside the kitchen until he gets to try a few tasters—still warm—of my new cookie creations. And I am sure he is grateful when I bake him a special treat now and then. So we both feel happy.

Of course, you can look at the baking of dog treats in a purely pragmatic manner. The home-made cookies are usually cheaper than bought ones, and they contain no preservatives or flavor enhancers. For children, baking cookies is an enjoyable way to pass the time, and adults can escape a little from their daily routine by kneading and shaping the dough.

The same applies to cookies and cakes as to all extra treats: too much is not good for your dog. It doesn't matter how healthy the ingredients are: they cannot and should not replace your dog's normal diet, only supplement it. If you care for your dog's health, then feed it cookies only in carefully measured quantities—and ignore that pleading, begging look in your dog's eyes.

Some things should never be included in dog treats: chemical additives, spicy seasoning, white sugar, chocolate, and cocoa should never be put in the dog bowl or into your baked dog treats. Apart from that, your creativity in baking need know few bounds. As our home-made cookies don't contain preservatives, they will not keep forever. We let a lot of the cookies dry out in the oven after baking, to let them harden. This means that the dogs have more fun chewing them and also, when biting, clean their teeth. For older dogs, take the cookies out of the oven straight away and let them cool on a rack.

Some tasty treats from the oven are intended to be eaten quickly. When we bake these recipes, we distribute them generously to all dogs that we like—even if my own dog Dexter is not exactly in favor of this rule.

Baking for your dog can make you and your dog happy and is easy, even for beginners. We had lots of fun in our kitchen and would like to take this opportunity to thank all dogs whose lip-smacking agreement or simple refusal of food has contributed to the quality of the dog treats in this book. A very special thank you is owed to my sister Monika and niece Julia. Not only did they bake all the cookies in many different variations, but also they tirelessly tested and further refined their creations in a circle of dog-loving friends.

Ingeborg Pils

TASTY TREATS FOR
LITTLE TREASURES

Linda's Liver Sausage Cookies

Makes about 40 cookies

3½ oz (100 g) coarse rolled oats
3½ oz (100 g) fine rolled oats
5 oz (150 g) farmer's cheese
3½ oz (100 g) liver sausage
6 tablespoons corn oil
1 egg

Mix all the ingredients to make a dough. It should not be too firm. If required, add a little extra water or flour.

Line a baking tray with baking parchment. Shape the dough into little balls, place them on the baking paper, and flatten them. Place them in the cold oven, set it to 350°F (180°C) (with fan), and bake for 30 minutes.

Let the liver sausage cookies cool on a wire rack. Keep them in a cookie tin. If your dog permits, the liver sausage cookies will keep for about 3 weeks.

HERBY FISH HEARTS

Makes about 35 hearts

3½ oz (100 g) cooked fish, without bones
3 tablespoons finely chopped fresh herbs
2 tablespoons extra virgin olive oil
1 egg
7 oz (200 g) spelt flour
3½ oz (100 g) ground hazelnuts

Purée the fish and the herbs in a food processor. Put the purée in a bowl, then stir in the olive oil and the egg. Add the flour and nuts, then mix all the ingredients to make a smooth dough. Shape the dough into a ball, wrap it in plastic wrap, and let it rest for 30 minutes.

Preheat the oven to 350°F (180°C). Line a baking tray with baking parchment.

On a floured surface, roll out the dough until about ¼ inch (8 mm) thick. With a cookie cutter, cut out little heart shapes. Place these on the baking tray and bake in the oven for 30 minutes.

Let the fish hearts cool on a wire rack. Store in a cookie tin; they will keep for about 2 weeks.

Dixie's Cheese Crunchies

Makes about 30 crunchies

3½ oz (100 g) chopped almonds
3½ oz (100 g) roughly chopped hazelnuts
5 oz (150 g) grated Emmental cheese
4 eggs
1 lb 3 oz (550 g) buckwheat flour
1 tablespoon honey
water and flour as required

Toast the almonds and hazelnuts in a non-stick pan, without oil or fat, until a light brown. Remove from the heat and let them cool.

Knead the nuts in with the remaining ingredients to form a smooth dough. If required, add a little more water or flour, depending on whether the dough is too dry or too moist.

Preheat the oven to 320°F (160°C). Line a baking sheet with baking parchment.

On a floured surface, roll out the dough to about ½ inch (1 cm) thick. Using a pastry wheel, cut into rectangles about ¾ inch x 2 inches (2 cm x 5 cm) in size.

Place the cookies on the baking sheet. Bake for 1 hour. Turn off the heat and let the cookies dry for another hour in the oven. Store in a paper or linen bag; they will keep for about 4 weeks.

BUTTERMILK SNACKS

Makes about 35 snacks

9 oz (250 g) chicken livers
1 tablespoon sunflower oil
3 fl oz (100 ml) buttermilk
9 oz (250 g) wholegrain spelt flour

Chop the liver very finely (use a food processor or meat grinder), then stir in the sunflower oil and buttermilk. Add the spelt flour and knead all the ingredients together to make a smooth dough. Cover the dough and let it rest in the refrigerator for 30 minutes.

Line a baking sheet with baking parchment.

On a floured surface, roll out the dough to about ½ inch (1 cm) thick. Use cookie cutters—any shape you like—to cut out shapes. Place the cookies on the baking sheet.

Bake the snacks at 350°F (180°C) (with fan) for 30 minutes. Turn off the oven and let the cookies dry in the oven for another hour. Store in a cookie tin. The snacks will keep for about 2 weeks.

PAULINE'S CHEESE DREAMS

Makes about 40 cheese dreams

4½ oz (125 g) farmer's cheese
2½ oz (75 g) grated Parmesan cheese
10½ oz (300 g) all-purpose flour
2 tablespoons wheatgerm oil
3½ oz (100 g) finely chopped hazelnuts

Preheat the oven to 400°F (200°C). Line a baking sheet with baking parchment.

Put all the ingredients into a bowl and mix well using the dough hooks on a hand-held mixer. Use 2 teaspoons to shape little portions of the dough and place the shapes on the baking sheet.

Bake the cookies for 30 minutes. Turn off the oven and let the cookies dry for another 2 hours in the oven. Store in a paper or linen bag. The cheese dreams will keep for about 4 weeks.

CRUNCHY PUMPKIN CRESCENTS

Makes about 35 crescents

3 potatoes, boiled unpeeled
5 oz (150 g) cooked pumpkin flesh
3½ oz (100 g) sausage meat
3½ oz (100 g) wholewheat flour
3 tablespoons pumpkin seed oil
1 egg
2 oz (50 g) pumpkin seeds

Peel the potatoes, then put them through a potato ricer. Purée the pumpkin flesh, and mix with the potato and sausage meat.

Add flour, oil, and the egg, then knead all the ingredients to make a smooth dough. Cover and let rest for 30 minutes.

Preheat the oven to 350°F (180°C). Line a baking sheet with baking parchment.

On a floured surface, roll out the dough until about ½ inch (1 cm) thick and use a cookie cutter to make crescent shapes. Place the cookies on the baking sheet and decorate with pumpkin seeds.

Bake the pumpkin crescents for 25 minutes. Turn off the heat and let the cookies dry in the oven for another 2 hours.

**"My dog is dearest to my heart,
Man says it is a sin,
My dog is true in the tempest of life,
And Man not even in the wind."**

St. Francis of Assisi

HEALTHY
BITES

BONNIE'S BANANA COOKIES

Makes about 30 cookies

2 carrots
1 banana
7 oz (200 g) all-purpose flour
3½ oz (100 g) fine rolled oats
1½ fl oz (50 ml) sunflower oil
water as required

Grate the carrots finely and mash the banana with a fork. Mix to make a dough with the flour, rolled oats, and oil. If necessary, add a little water.

Preheat the oven to 350°F (180°C). Line a baking sheet with baking parchment.

On a floured surface, roll out the dough to about ½ inch (1 cm) thick and cut squares about 1½ inches (4 cm) in size. Place these on the sheet and bake for 25 minutes. Turn off the heat and let them cool overnight in the oven. Store in a paper or linen bag. The cookies will keep for about 3 weeks.

SAMMY'S ANCHOVY PURSES

Makes about 15 purses

5 oz (150 g) soft cream cheese
3 tablespoons milk
2 tablespoons fish oil
4 tablespoons safflower oil
11 oz (300 g) wholewheat flour
15 anchovy fillets
3½ oz (100 g) farmer's cheese
1 egg white

Stir the cream cheese into the milk, fish oil, and safflower oil. Gradually stir in half the flour into the cheese mixture, then knead in the rest. Cover the dough and let it rest for 30 minutes.

Preheat the oven to 400°F (200°C). Line a baking sheet with baking parchment.

On a floured surface, roll out the dough and cut out 30 circles with a cookie cutter. Rinse the anchovy fillets in cold water, then place them on half the dough circles and cover each with some of the farmer's cheese. Paint the edges of the circles with the egg white. Cover with the remaining circles and press the edges firmly together.

Place the dough purses on the baking sheet and bake for 25 minutes. Turn off the heat and let them dry in the oven. Store in a cookie tin.

The anchovy purses will keep for about 5 days.

APPLE AND CARROT DUMPLINGS

Makes about 40 dumplings

1 apple
1 carrot
5 oz (150 g) spelt flour
5 oz (150 g) coarse rolled oats
2 eggs
3 tablespoons molasses
water and flour as required

Finely grate the apple and carrot, then mix with the other ingredients to make an easily shaped dough. If necessary, add a little extra water or flour.

Preheat the oven to 350°F (180°C). Line a baking sheet with baking parchment.

Use 2 teaspoons to shape the mixture into little dumplings and place the dumplings on the baking sheet. Bake for 30 minutes, then turn off the heat and let the dumplings dry in the oven. Store in a paper or linen bag. The dumplings will keep for about 3 weeks.

TOFU STRIPS À LA TIFFANY

Makes about 35 strips

7 oz (200 g) tofu
3 carrots
3 tablespoons corn oil
2 eggs
9 oz (250 g) wholewheat flour
1 tablespoon rosemary leaflets

Crumble the tofu and grate the carrots. Purée in a blender with the corn oil. Knead the eggs and flour into the purée. Chop the rosemary leaflets and knead them into the dough.

Preheat the oven to 350°F (180°C). Line a baking sheet with baking parchment.

On a floured surface, roll out the dough to about ¼ inch (5 mm) thick and use a pastry wheel to cut strips about ¾ inch x 2¾ inches (2 cm x 7 cm). Place on the baking sheet and bake for 30 minutes. Turn the strips halfway through the baking time.

Let the tofu strips cool on a wire rack. Store in a cookie tin. The strips will keep for about 2 weeks.

BENJI'S RICE CRACKERS

Makes about 35 crackers

3 small zucchini
11 oz (300 g) cooked short-grain rice
7 oz (200 g) soft cream cheese
1 egg
7 oz (200 g) wholewheat flour

Finely grate the zucchini. Mix them with the rice, cream cheese, and egg, then gradually work in the flour.

Preheat the oven to 400°F (200°C). Line a baking tray with baking parchment.

On a floured surface, roll out the dough to about ¾ inch (2 cm) thick and cut it into 1½ inch (4 cm) squares. Place the squares on the baking sheet and bake for 40 minutes. Then turn off the heat and let the crackers dry out overnight in the oven. Store in a paper or linen bag. The crackers will keep for about 2 weeks.

DEXTER'S SPINACH COOKIES

Makes about 40 cookies

4½ oz (125 g) deep frozen spinach
2 tablespoons grated Parmesan cheese
3½ oz (100 g) all-purpose flour
3½ oz (100 g) fine rolled oats
water and flour as required

Cook the spinach in a little water, then drain it thoroughly and purée in a blender. Mix the spinach purée with the remaining ingredients to make an easily shaped dough. If necessary, add a little water or flour.

Preheat the oven to 350°F (180°C). Line a baking sheet with baking parchment.

Shape little portions of the dough with a spoon and place them on the baking sheet. Bake in the oven for about 30 minutes.

Let the spinach cookies cool on a wire tray and store in a cookie tin. The cookies will keep for about 2 weeks.

HEARTY
NIBBLES

PIPPA'S TRIPE COOKIES

Makes about 40 cookies

6 fl oz (200 ml) hot water
7 oz (200 g) polenta
3½ oz (100 g) cornflour
2 oz (50 g) tripe, finely chopped
1 egg

Pour the hot water over the polenta, stir and let cool. Then knead in the other ingredients.

Preheat the oven to 350°F (180°C). Line a baking sheet with baking paper.

On a floured surface, roll out the dough to about ½ inch (1 cm) thick and cut it into triangles. Place these on the baking sheet and bake for 25 minutes. Turn off the heat and let the cookies dry for a few hours in the oven. Store in a screw-topped glass jar or in a cookie tin. The cookies will keep for about 4 weeks.

CRUNCHY SESAME BITES

Makes about 30 bites

9 oz (250 g) spelt flour
3½ oz (100 g) grated Emmental cheese
3 oz (80 g) low fat cream cheese
2 eggs
1 oz (30 g) sesame seeds

Knead all the ingredients, except for the sesame seeds, together to form an easily shaped dough. Make small, thumb-sized rolls from the dough and press one side into the sesame seeds.

Preheat the oven to 350°F (180°C). Line a baking sheet with baking parchment.

Place the sesame bites on the baking sheet and bake for 30 minutes. Turn off the heat and leave the bites to dry overnight in the oven. Store in a paper or linen bag. The sesame bites will keep for about 3 weeks.

REWARD COOKIES

Makes about 35 cookies

3½ oz (100 g) wholewheat flour
3½ oz (100 g) coarse rolled oats
2 tablespoons oat bran
2 eggs
2½ oz (75 g) grated Parmesan cheese
2½ oz (75 g) finely diced ham
3 fl oz (100 ml) water

Mix all the ingredients with the water to make a smooth dough. Cover and let the dough rest for about 30 minutes.

Preheat the oven to 350°F (180°C). Line a baking sheet with baking parchment.

On a floured surface, roll out the dough to about ½ inch (1 cm) thick and cut into 1¼ x 2 inch (3 cm x 5 cm) rectangles. Place these on the baking sheet and bake for 25 minutes. Turn off the heat and let the cookies harden in the oven for another 2 hours. Store in a paper or linen bag. The cookies will keep for about 4 weeks.

"As long as human beings think that animals do not feel, animals have to feel that human beings cannot think."

Arthur Schopenhauer

SAMANTHA'S SCONES

Makes about 12 scones

5 oz (150 g) all-purpose flour
1 egg
3½ oz (100 g) wholegrain spelt flour
3 teaspoons baking powder
1 teaspoon seaweed powder
1 tablespoon brewer's yeast
5 fl oz (150 ml) milk
½ stick (50 g) butter

Knead all the ingredients to make a smooth dough. Let the dough rest for 10 minutes. Preheat the oven to 400°F (200°C). Line a baking sheet with baking parchment.

On a floured surface, roll out the dough to about ¾ inch (2 cm) thick and cut out round cookie shapes with a glass about 2 inches (5 cm) in diameter. Place the shapes on the baking tray and bake for 10 minutes.

Let the scones cool on a wire tray.

BOBBY'S BROWNIES

Makes about 30 brownies

7 oz (200 g) wholewheat flour
7 oz (200 g) spelt flour
3½ oz (100 g) chopped walnuts
2 eggs
2 tablespoons sunflower oil
2 tablespoons molasses
½ sachet of dried yeast
water and flour as required

In a food processor, mix all the ingredients to form a firm dough. If necessary, add a little extra flour or water. Shape the dough into a ball and let it rise in a warm spot for 1 hour.

Preheat the oven to 320°F (160°C). Line a shallow rectangular baking pan with baking parchment.

Spread the dough over the baking pan until about 1½ inches (4 cm) thick. Bake for 35 minutes, then let it cool for 1 hour, still in the baking pan.

Turn out the baked cake, with the baking parchment, onto a board. Remove the baking parchment and cut the cake into dog bite-sized pieces. Store in a paper or linen bag. The brownies will keep for about 4 weeks.

MUESLI ROLLS

Makes about 30 rolls

1 apple
1 pear
3½ oz (100 g) all-purpose flour
3½ oz (100 g) coarse rolled oats
2½ oz (75 g) chopped hazelnuts
1 tablespoon honey
3½ oz (100 g) cream
2 oz (50 g) flax seeds

Roughly grate the apple and pear. Mix with the other ingredients, except for the flax seeds. With a tablespoon, take little portions of the dough and make roll shapes.

Preheat the oven to 350°F (180°C). Line a baking sheet with baking parchment.

Roll the muesli rolls in the flax seeds, place them on the baking tray, and flatten them. Bake for 30 minutes, then turn off the heat and let the rolls cool in the oven. Store in a paper or linen bag. The muesli rolls will keep for about 3 weeks.

51

CHEWY FUN
FOR
GREAT FRIENDS

SCAMP'S GROUND BEEF COOKIES

Makes about 20 cookies

11 oz (300 g) wholewheat flour
2 tablespoons mixed dried herbs
2 tablespoons safflower oil
1 egg
2½ oz (75 g) peeled sunflower seeds
5 fl oz (150 ml) water

Preheat the oven to 400°F (200°C). Line a baking sheet with baking parchment.

Mix all the ingredients except for the sunflower seeds with 5 fl oz (150 ml) water to make a dough. On a floured surface, roll out the pastry to about 1 inch (2 cm) thick and cut it into 1¼ x 2¼ inch (3 cm x 6 cm) rectangles. Press one side into the sunflower seeds and place with the other side downward onto the baking sheet.

Bake the cookies for 40 minutes. Turn off the heat and let the cookies harden overnight in the oven. Store in a cookie tin. The cookies will keep for around 2 weeks.

WILLY'S WHEAT CRESCENTS

Makes about 35 crescents

3½ oz (100 g) all-purpose flour
5 oz (150 g) wholewheat flour
3½ oz (100 g) wheatgerm
3 tablespoons sunflower oil
8½ fl oz (250 ml) unsalted vegetable stock
2½ oz (75 g) cracked wheat

Mix both types of flour, the wheatgerm, and the oil,
pour on the stock, and mix to make a smooth dough.
Cover the dough and let it rest for 20 minutes.

Preheat the oven to 400°F (200°C). Line a baking sheet with baking parchment.

Form the dough into a long roll and cut into slices. Shape the slices into balls,
then roll them into sausage shapes and wind them around your forefinger
to form crescents. Roll them in the cracked wheat and place them on the
baking sheet.

Bake for 30 minutes. Turn off the heat and let the crescents dry out in the oven
for another 2 hours. Store in a paper or linen bag. The crescents will keep for about
4 weeks.

Gina's Polenta Cookies with Liver Sausage

Makes about 40 cookies

8½ fl oz (250 ml) water
5 oz (150 g) polenta
5 oz (150 g) cornflour
3½ oz (100 g) canned corn kernels, drained
3½ oz (100 g) coarse liver sausage
2 oz (50 g) lard
1 egg

Bring the water to the boil. Mix the polenta with the water and let it soak. When the polenta has cooled, mix with the remaining ingredients.

Preheat the oven to 350°F (180°C). Line a baking sheet with baking parchment.

On a floured surface, roll out the dough to about ¾ inch (2 cm) thick and cut out circles with a cookie cutter. Place these on the baking sheet and bake for 30 minutes. Turn off the heat and let the cookies harden overnight in the oven. Store in a screw-topped glass jar or a cookie tin. The cookies will keep for about 2 weeks.

CRISPY BACON ROLLS

Makes about 30 rolls

5 oz (150 g) wholewheat flour
5 oz (150 g) wholegrain rye flour
2½ oz (75 g) wheat grains
2½ oz (75 g) bacon cubes
1 tablespoon brewer's yeast
3 tablespoons safflower oil
8½ fl oz (250 ml) unsalted meat stock
2½ oz (75 g) cracked wheat

Thoroughly mix all the ingredients except for the cracked wheat. Cover the dough and let it rest for 30 minutes.

Preheat the oven to 350°F (180°C). Line a baking sheet with baking parchment.

Take portions of the dough with a large spoon and shape into rolls. Roll them in the cracked wheat. Place them on the baking sheet and bake for 45 minutes. Turn off the heat and let them dry in the oven until they are quite hard. Store in a paper or linen bag. The rolls will keep for about 3 weeks.

BILLY'S CRUNCHY BONES

Makes about 6 "bones"

1 bunch watercress
14 oz (400 g) wholewheat flour
3½ oz (100 g) coarse rolled oats
2 oz (50 g) wheatgerm
2 oz (50 g) peeled sunflower seeds
2 oz (50 g) lard
8½ fl oz (250 ml) unsalted meat stock

Finely chop the watercress. Knead it in with the other ingredients to form a dough. Roll out the dough to a thickness of about ¾ inch (2 cm) and cut out 6 bone-shaped pieces with a sharp knife.

Preheat the oven to 350°F (180°C). Line a baking sheet with baking parchment.

Place the "bones" on the baking tray and bake for 45 minutes. Turn off the heat and let the bone shapes dry in the oven overnight. Store in a paper or linen bag. The "bones" will keep for about 2 weeks.

BELLA'S ALMOND CANTUCCINI

Makes about 40 cantuccini

7 oz (200 g) cornflour
3½ oz (100 g) chopped almonds
1 egg
1 tablespoon honey
1 tablespoon extra virgin olive oil
1 tablespoon molasses
water as required

Knead all the ingredients together to make a smooth dough, adding a little water
if required. Shape the dough into a roll, wrap it in plastic wrap, and let it rest for
1 hour in the refrigerator.

Preheat the oven to 350°F (180°C). Line a baking sheet with baking parchment.

Cut the roll of dough into slices about ½ inch (1 cm) thick and place these on the
baking sheet. Bake for about 30 minutes in the preheated oven, then turn off
the heat and let the cantuccini dry in the oven. Store in a paper or linen bag. The
cantuccini will keep for about 4 weeks.

EXTRA TREATS FOR GREEDY GOURMETS

CHRISTMAS SAUSAGE COOKIES

Makes about 30 cookies

9 oz (250 g) whole grain rye flour
3½ oz (100 g) rolled oats
1 oz (30 g) lard
3½ oz (100 g) sausage meat
6 fl oz (200 ml) water

Mix the ingredients with the water and knead them to make a firm dough. Shape the dough into a ball, wrap it in plastic wrap, and let it rest in the refrigerator for 30 minutes.

Preheat the oven to 320°F (160°C). Line a baking sheet with baking parchment.

On a floured surface, roll out the dough to a thickness of about ½ inch (1 cm) and use a cookie cutter to cut out cookie shapes. Place these on the baking sheet and bake for 40 minutes. Turn off the heat and let the cookies dry in the oven. Store in a cookie tin. The cookies will keep for about 2 weeks.

GUS'S POULTRY NIBBLES

Makes about 30 nibbles

14 oz (400 g) chicken or turkey breast

Cut the meat into thin strips with a sharp knife. Preheat the oven to 300°F (150°C).

Line a baking sheet with baking parchment and place the strips of meat on it side by side. Roast in the oven for 30–40 minutes.

Reduce the oven temperature to 210°F (100°C) and wedge a wooden spoon in the oven door to let the moisture escape. Let the strips of meat dry out for another 2 hours in the oven. Remove the baking sheet and let the strips of meat finish drying out overnight at room temperature. Keep in the refrigerator. The strips will keep for about 4 days.

MIMI'S MUESLI MUFFINS

Makes 24 muffins

9 oz (250 g) rolled oats
3½ oz (100 g) wholewheat flour
4½ oz (125 g) cracked wheat
2 tablespoons oat germ
3 teaspoons baking powder
3 tablespoons maple syrup
1 egg
2 bananas
3½ oz (100 g) blueberries
3 fl oz (100 ml) water

And also:
2 mini-muffin sheets, each for 12 muffins

Knead all the ingredients (except for the fruit) together to make a dough. Mash the bananas with a fork and mix into the dough. Finally, mix in the blueberries.

Preheat the oven to 350°F (180°C).

Distribute the dough among the molds in the mini-muffin sheet and bake for 30 minutes. Tip out the muffins onto a wire rack and let them cool. Store in a cookie tin. The muffins will keep for about 4 days.

SUSIE'S JUICY CHRISTMAS CAKES

Makes 6 cakes

9 oz (250 g) dried fruit (no raisins)
A little lukewarm water
9 oz (250 g) hazelnuts
3½ oz (100 g) unsweetened dried coconut flakes
2 tablespoons molasses
2 eggs
4½ oz (125 g) wholewheat flour
2 tablespoons breadcrumbs

Soak the dried fruit for 30 minutes in the water. Then pour into a sieve, drain well, and chop coarsely. Mix the dried fruit with the other ingredients to make a dough and let it rest for 30 minutes.

Preheat the oven to 350°F (180°C).

Divide the dough into 6 portions. Shape into round, flat little cakes and place these on a baking sheet. Bake for 40 minutes, then tip them onto a wire rack for cooling. Store in a cookie tin. The cakes will keep for about 2 weeks.

TOBY'S TUNA TRIANGLES

Makes about 40 triangles

1 can tuna fish in natural juice
4 tablespoons extra virgin olive oil
1 egg
1 teaspoon dried thyme
1 teaspoon dried oregano
9 oz (250 g) cornflour
5 oz (150 g) rolled oats
2 oz (50 g) flour

Drain the tuna in a sieve, then purée it with the oil and the egg in a blender.
Mix the purée with the other ingredients to make a dough.

Preheat the oven to 350°F (180°C). Line a baking sheet with baking parchment.

Roll out the dough to about ½ inch (1 cm) thick and cut it into triangles. Place the cookies on the baking sheet and bake for 25 minutes. Store in a cookie tin. The triangles will keep for about 2 weeks.

FREDA'S FINE BIRTHDAY FISH TARTS

Makes 6 tarts

11 oz (300 g) pearl barley
water
7 oz (200 g) cooked fillet of fish
1 egg
2 tablespoons corn starch
2 tablespoons finely chopped mixed herbs

And also:
6 non-stick small tart molds 5 inches (12 cm)
in diameter

Soak the pearl barley for 35 minutes in the water, then drain well in a sieve.

Preheat the oven to 350°F (180°C).

Break up the fish fillet into small pieces with a fork and mix it with the pearl barley, egg, corn starch, and herbs. Divide the dough into 6 portions, put these into the tart molds, and bake for 40 minutes. Then turn off the heat and let the tarts cool in their molds in the oven. Store in a cookie tin. The tarts will keep for about 3 days.

Picture credits
Corbis: I William Geddes/Beateworks, 6 Flint, 21 DLILLC,
22 Ursula Klawitter/zefa, 36 Ursula Klawitter/zefa,
46 BreBa/bilderlounge, 52 Grove Pashly/Brand X,
66 Ursula Klawitter/zefa